30 DAYS

OF BRUTAL HONESTY

ACILLEN K. WATTS

30 Days of Brutal Honesty

Copyright © 2021 by Acillen K. Watts

Contact us at www.chosenwarrior17@gmail.com

www. acillen.com

Illustration Credit:

Sienna Napoleon Illustration /Book Cover

DEDICATION

This book is dedicated to all the amazing people I have met along this journey. I thank God for revelations and teachings that could only have come from Him. I dedicate this journal to all the Chosen Warriors who have weathered the storm and are on their way to victory. I applaud your commitment to yourself and this journey. This book is dedicated to all the readers who are bold and brave enough to tackle the darkness in order to find the light in their lives. This book is dedicated to you. Yes, YOU with love.

TABLE OF CONTENTS

INTRODUCTION

It is time to let go. I am excited to present this opportunity for you to break free from chains of bondage. This book is designed for you to face your pain, defeat the enemy, and claim victory in your life. On each day, you will tackle one struggle that many people have faced but never truly overcame. Each day you will go to a quiet place to write down your truth. As you write on the pages, the pain within will be forced to come out. The spiritual chains around your mind and life will be broken. You will face truths you have never faced and attack demons that have ruled in your life for far too long. This book and your pen will serve as a weapon of mass destruction against the enemy. It is time to take back your life and become a true warrior.

For this process to be effective, you must commit to being brutally honest with yourself. The truth will set you free. Whether you take this 30-day journey alone or with a friend, take it. Healing will come. After you tackle the subject and burn the pages each day, you will be left with something incredibly special. What you are left with will change your perspective and therefore change your life.

WARNING: Be sure to burn the pages where you will not cause harm to property, yourself, or anyone else. Use caution around flammable objects.

DAY ONE

PAIN

Everyone has experienced pain. Some have experienced a lifetime of hurt and pain. When you think of the word pain as it relates to your life, what person comes to mind? What did they do to you? What did their actions or words take from you? What did you do with the pain they caused?

____

____

____

____

____

____

____

____

____

____

____

PRAY:

Father God, I release my pain to you. I forgive the person who caused this pain that cut so deep. It will no longer have power in my life. I command the enemy to leave my life in Jesus's name. I burn my past and trust my life to you now and forever. In the mighty name of Jesus, I pray. Amen. CUT THEN BURN THESE PAGES.

DAY 2

SECRET SINS

Everyone has SECRETS. Some secrets torment us whether they are about us or someone else. What secret are you hiding that torments you? What is a secret you think about and can't tell anyone? What makes you feel guilt, shame, or fear of anyone knowing?

____

____

____

____

____

____

____

____

____

____

____

____

PRAY:

Father God, I humbly repent for my sin. I ask that you cleanse me of all unrighteousness. I bind any unclean spirits in me and any coming against me under the blood of Jesus. I forgive myself and cast out the spirit of guilt, shame, and fear in my life. I burn the memory of secrets and usher the spirit of truth into my life. In Jesus's mighty name, I pray. Amen. CUT THEN BURN THESE PAGES.

DAY 3

DEPRESSION

Everyone feels sadness, but having depression means something more wicked is at work. It sits in the deepest valleys of your mind and steals your joy. There are triggers for depression. Most of the time one bad thought leads to another. They consume you and trigger emotions you cannot control. You shut down, shut people out, or worse. What thoughts cause you to feel seriously depressed or even suicidal? Why do you feel the devil torments you with those specific thoughts?

____

____

____

____

____

____

____

PRAY:

Father God, I command the spirit of depression to leave my body now! I plead the blood of Jesus over my mind and body. I cast down evil thoughts to the pit of hell and command the spirit of peace to guard my thoughts. I praise you Lord for the victory. In Jesus's mighty name, I pray. Amen. CUT THEN BURN THESE PAGES.

DAY 4

ILLNESS/SICKNESS

Every sickness starts with the presence of a spirit that dwells within us. If people can be healed in the spirit, they can be made sick by a spirit. The spirit of sickness is an evil thief that attacks even the most innocent. Who has the spirit of sickness/infirmity attacked and left broken in your life? How did it make you feel? What did it take from you emotionally, physically, and spiritually? Did you get angry with God?

____

____

____

____

____

____

____

____

____

____

____

PRAY:

Father God, I release these negative feelings now. I ask forgiveness for any anger and blame I placed on you. Father, I speak life and call upon the warring spirit of wellbeing to fight against sickness. I speak healing into the circumstances and choose to trust you, Lord. In Jesus's mighty name, I pray. Amen. CUT THEN BURN THESE PAGES.

DAY 5

DISAPPOINTMENT

Life is full of disappointments. We feel let down by ourselves, other people, even God. We hope and pray but sometimes do not see any significant changes, things do not happen the way we hoped, or nothing happens at all. Sometimes we lack the courage to say who and what let us down, but it hurts to the core. People can disappoint us by not supporting us, not being loyal or honest, not protecting us, and in so many other ways. When it happens, scars and wounds are left. Tell the truth. Who disappointed you? What did they do? What happened to you because of what they did? Did it cause long-term damage?

____

____

____

____

____

____

____

____

____

____

PRAY:

Father God, I pray against the spirit of disappointment. I forgive myself and anyone who has disappointed me. I ask that you restore me. Father, strengthen me and place in me the power to control any actions or emotions that would work against me. Set me free from the bondage of depression. In the mighty name of Jesus, I pray. Amen. CUT THEN BURN THESE PAGES.

DAY 6

REJECTION

Rejection stings. Someone or some circumstance is saying you do not measure up, don't belong, and don't matter. It is hard to take someone saying that nothing about you is acceptable, especially when you cannot do anything about it. Someone rejecting your love, kindness, ideas, personality, and appearance hurts. It leaves you feeling worthless, small, irrelevant, and not good enough. This can lead to self-doubt and the need to "prove yourself" rather than just being free to be who you are. What rejection had the worst impact on your life? Who did it? What happened? What did it do to you? Let it out and let it go.

____

____

____

____

____

____

____

____

____

PRAY:

Father God, I rebuke and bind the spirit of rejection. I choose to believe what you say about me. You approved me when you gave me life. I am here because you saved me for your perfect will. I love who you made me to be and honor you with my life. I embrace every imperfection. In Jesus's mighty name, I pray. Amen. CUT THEN BURN THESE PAGES

DAY 7

ABUSE

It was wrong. Whether you were the abuser or the one being physically, sexually, or mentally abused, it was pure evil. Abuse kills, steals, and destroys. It wounds the soul so deeply many never return to who they were before the abuse happened. Innocence, self-confidence, and self-respect are snatched through the abuse. Face the abuse right now. Pull it up from the depths of your soul so it no longer has power over your life. *Write it down.* The enemy can't torment you about what they did or what you did any longer. Face it and claim the victory. You are an overcomer.

____

____

____

____

____

____

35

PRAY:

Father God, I forgive my abuser (I forgive myself for being an abuser). Father take from me this cross I bear from the weight of the attack against me. Cleanse my mind of ALL thoughts and memories associated with abuse. I rebuke the evil spirits and release this pain to you right now in the name of Jesus. It will no longer have power in my life. The enemy is defeated. Victory is mine. Guard my heart and mind against the enemy in Jesus's name. I burn the past and trust my life to you now and forever. Amen. CUT THEN BURN THESE PAGES.

DAY 8

ENVY

Envy towards another person is never good. It can cause you to pull away from someone or reject someone who could be a good friend or blessing in your life. Envy is a personal hang-up that causes you to be judgmental and leaves you feeling inferior. Admitting the real issue is YOUR ENVY takes courage. *Talk about who you envy and why here.* Why do they make you feel so bad about yourself? Let it go and stop comparing your life to theirs. Embrace who you are and commit to meeting the best version of yourself. Time to conquer your envy. Write it out.

____

____

____

____

____

____

____

____

____

____

____

PRAY:

Father God, I rebuke the spirit of envy from my life. Help me to love myself and who you created me to be. Father help me to see myself through your eyes. Help me to walk in love, not hate, and to be a light in this world no matter how I feel personally. Open my heart right now Lord. In Jesus's mighty name, I pray. Amen. CUT THEN BURN THESE PAGES.

DAY 9

SELF-DOUBT

Why is it so hard for you to believe in yourself? There are things you want to do and love to do, but self-doubt is stopping you. Did someone make you think you couldn't do it? Maybe they made you feel bad about your ideas or picked on you and made you question yourself. Let go of self-doubt today. If you can speak it and believe it, you can achieve it in God. Write down the things you doubt about yourself. Stop the cycle. Walk in faith and rebuke the negative thoughts every time they come.

____

____

____

____

____

____

____

____

____

____

PRAY:

Father God, I know that through Christ I can do all things. I am limited only when I believe the lies of the devil. I rebuke the spirit of self-doubt in my life and denounce all negative thoughts that play in my head. I declare victory and power in the mighty name of Jesus. I choose to believe and love myself. In Jesus's mighty name, I pray. Amen. CUT THEN BURN THESE PAGES.

DAY 10

FEAR

Fear is gripping and hides behind arrogance and rejection. People say they don't want something for fear of never getting it. How is fear stopping you? What do you fear most? Most of the things we fear are associated with our thoughts. Most of what we think will happen never does. The only thing you should fear is allowing fear and worry to rule your life. It's time to let the fear go and walk in faith. Write down what you fear most. Write down those negative thoughts and make the decision today to push forward AT ANY COST.

____

____

____

____

____

____

———————————————————————

———————————————————————

51

———————————————————————

———————————————————————

PRAY:

Father God, I rebuke the spirit of fear. Father, I ask that you remove the unclean spirit of fear from me. I thank you for boldness and courage this day. Father help me to fight when I want to quit and to push past my fear to accomplish your will for my life. In Jesus's mighty name, I pray. Amen. CUT THEN BURN THESE PAGES.

DAY 11

SHAME

Shame often accompanies some form of guilt. We all make mistakes and get it wrong, but some things we do eat away at us. When we make bad choices even with good intentions, they can lead to circumstances that make us feel ashamed. Shame hurts. You cannot let shame win. You must forgive yourself and do better in the future. Did anger, low self-esteem, loneliness, or any other emotion lead you to do something you are ashamed of now? Write it down and let it go today.

____

____

____

____

____

____

____

____

____

____

PRAY:

Father God, please forgive me of my sin. I humbly repent for anything I have done that has brought shame into my life. Please help me to love and forgive myself today. Lord, I rebuke the spirit of fear and shame. I invite confidence and self-love into my life. Use me Lord in a mighty way. I burn the past and trust my life to you now and forever. In Jesus's mighty name, I pray. Amen. BURN THESE PAGES.

DAY 12

SELF HATE/LOATHING

Why is it so hard for you to love yourself? Why do you look at yourself through the world's warped lens versus the eyes of God? Essentially, you are telling God you do not like His creation. Instead of loving yourself, you have allowed other people to determine your worth. It is called "self" confidence for a reason. It is not "their' confidence. It is time to stop hating things about yourself. If you can do something about what you don't like, then do it. If not, stop the madness. Write down what you hate about yourself even if it is something you did in your past. Get it out, face it, and be free today.

____

____

____

____

____

____

____

____

____

PRAY:

Father God, please help me love myself. I rebuke the spirit of hatred and welcome self-love. Lord, I repent for complaining instead of focusing on the wins in my life. Help me to love who I see in the mirror and learn to have joy in all things. I ask you to remove from my life anyone who condemns or criticizes me to hurt me. I reject evil words spoken to break me. I command the self-condemning spirit of the enemy to leave now. In the mighty name of Jesus, I pray. Amen. CUT THEN BURN THESE PAGES.

DAY 13

REGRET

Some people say it is not good to regret. They say they would not change a thing about their lives, not even the bad things that happened because they help to make them who they are. That all sounds good, but regret is real. Many are sad and live in shame because of regrets. They wonder how their lives would be if they had not made certain wrong choices. Dwelling on things won't help, but being brutally honest about them will. Write down your deepest regrets and rid your mind and life of them for good. Shut them out and don't look back. You regret it and that is your truth. Now let go.

____

____

____

____

____

____

____

____

____

____

PRAY:

Father God, I humbly ask your forgiveness for the things I regret in my life. Father, please help me to make better choices and to seek you for guidance and wisdom in all things. I forgive myself and release all regrets I feel right now. I trust you Father with my present and my future. In Jesus's mighty name, I pray. Amen. CUT THEN BURN THESE PAGES.

DAY 14

HATEFUL WORDS

The words we say in anger cut like a knife. Words that come from our mouths can cripple others for years. Millions of human beings walk around replaying the terrible things people have said to them in their heads. We must stop letting the enemy use us to break or bruise another person because we have no self-control. What words did you say to someone else that were from the devil himself simply because of your anger, hurt, or pain? Write down the awful words you have spoken and any hateful things you have spoken about yourself. Forgive and stop the bleeding. If hateful words were said to you. Write them out of your soul.

____

____

____

____

____

____

____

____

____

PRAY:

Father God, please forgive my hateful words. Father, I ask that you reverse the impact of any hateful words that have come out of my mouth or penetrated my ears. I pray for self-discipline when I speak and when I am angry. Help me to handle myself in a manner that is pleasing to you. Lord, don't let me be a vessel for the enemy to use. I thank you in advance for all you are doing and have done for me. In Jesus's mighty name, I pray. Amen. CUT THEN BURN THESE PAGES.

DAY 15

LIES, LIES, LIES

What was the lie? Did you tell the lie, or did someone lie to you? Lies have severe consequences and can put a wedge between people that sometimes cannot be removed. A lie is a lie, tiny or big. If you lie to yourself to avoid the truth, it still makes you a liar. Write down the lies that were told to you that broke your heart or changed your life. Write down the lies you have told to others and write down the reason why you felt the need to lie to them. Process the *WHY's*, change your perception, and walk in your truth starting now.

____

____

____

____

____

PRAY:

Father God, I humbly ask your forgiveness for not being honest. I command the spirit of lying to leave my body now, in the name of Jesus. Cleanse me of all unrighteousness and help me to align my life with your Word. I choose to let go and forgive the people who have lied to me and give my heart to you right now Father. In Jesus's mighty name, I pray. Amen. CUT THEN BURN THESE PAGES.

DAY 16

SADNESS

Sadness is a real emotion and is common to man. We all have felt sadness at some point in our lives, even if it were from watching a sad movie. The problem comes into play when we live in sadness for too long. Loss of a loved one, relationship, illness, or a job can result in severe sadness. Sometimes we get sad when we think about people we love and all their poor choices. At times, we may feel sad when we think about our lives and all that has not happened. What makes you feel sad inside? What heartbreak have you struggled to move forward from, but cannot seem to get over it? Talk about it here so you can let it go for good.

____

____

____

____

____

PRAY:

Father God, I give to you my sadness today. No longer will I let sadness rule in my life. Father God please place a hedge of protection around my mind and heal my heart. Father, strengthen me when the actions of others cause me to feel sadness. Let your peace overtake me. In Jesus's mighty name, I pray. Amen. CUT THEN BURN THESE PAGES.

Acillen K. Watts

DAY 17

JUDGEMENT

Do you fear being judged by others? Does that fear stifle you and keep you from speaking your truth and doing things you want to do? Are you gripped with fear of what might be said about you by mere man or is there more to this stronghold in your life? When God is first in your life, you will focus on what He says, not man. Think about what is behind the fear. Do you fear them thinking less of you? Do you fear failing or not being enough? If you do, why? It is time to write it down and get it out of your life.

____

____

____

____

____

____

____

____

____

PRAY:

Father God, I rebuke and cast down the spirit of judgment. Please forgive my desire to honor man over you. Father help me to speak and act in confidence with you as my guide and protector. Give me the confidence to speak my truth with authority and not feel anxious about sharing myself with the world for your Glory. Help me to be a vessel that is pleasing to you Lord. In Jesus's mighty name, I pray. Amen. CUT THEN BURN THESE PAGES.

DAY 18

GUILT

Did you do it on purpose? Did you do it in ignorance and now wish you had made another choice? Were you in a dark place when you made that decision or let someone down? Are you tormenting yourself for not doing something only God has the power to do? If you have repented and ask God to forgive you, He has. He is no longer holding it, so why are you? It is time to be free of shame and guilt of doing wrong and align your life with the Word of God. Write it down and get it out. Forgive yourself.

____

____

____

____

____

____

____

____

____

PRAY:

Father God, I dedicate my life to you. I invite you to rule and reign in my life. I forgive myself and let go of the pains of my past. I ask for the wisdom to recognize and war against the tricks of the enemy in my life. I let go of guilt and rebuke that spirit in the mighty name of Jesus. It will no longer have power in my life. In Jesus's mighty name, I pray. Amen. CUT THEN BURN THESE PAGES.

DAY 19

SEXUAL SIN

Sexual sin is life-changing. When we have sex with people, we become one with them spiritually. You take on the spirits within them and they take on the spirits within you. In many cases, these spirits change our physical and mental make-up. Having sex outside of marriage is a sin. In some cases, sexual sin exists within marriage, especially with those who are led by the spirit of lust. People have stained what God intended. Write down the names of the people you have had sinful sex with throughout your life. Repent and forgive yourself. Pray for God to release you from any strongholds established through those acts.

____

____

____

____

____

____

____

____

____

____

PRAY:

Father God, forgive me for all sexual sin against you. Lord break any soul ties established from my fornication. I surrender my life to you and rebuke any demons I let into my life through sexual acts. Lord, please cleanse me of all unrighteousness and cover me in the blood of Jesus. I denounce demonic darkness in my life and detach my being from demonic strongholds established through sex. In Jesus's mighty name, I pray. Amen. CUT THEN BURN THESE PAGES.

DAY 20

GOSSIP

Gossip is one of the most common sins that slides under the radar. People glorify the work of the enemy without realizing that is what they are doing. Sharing bad news and saying mean things about people is terrible. Even sharing information that is true in the wrong manner can be gossip. Gossip hurts and leaves scars on those whose troubles are exposed and talked about. Guard your words and be mindful of what you share and with whom. When others lure you into gossip, resist and walk away. What have you gossiped about? What did you talk about that you should not have? What gossip loophole did you create for the enemy to come into your life?

____

____

____

____

____

____

PRAY:

Father God, I rebuke the spirit of gossip in my life. I ask forgiveness for any time I gossiped even unknowingly. Please help me to guard my heart, mind, and my words in the name of Jesus. Father cleanse me and help my actions to be pleasing unto you. Please reverse the negative impact of anything I have said and shared about myself or another person. In Jesus's mighty name, I pray. Amen. CUT THEN BURN THESE PAGES.

DAY 21

OFFENSE

How many times have you rejected the truth because you were offended? Do you find yourself offended often by something someone said to you or someone else? Do you possess unwarranted offenses on behalf of yourself and others because of past experiences? Stop being so offended. You could literally miss God or an opportunity because you are controlled by your emotions and always feel that you are being attacked. Write down the things that you find most offensive. Reflect and ask yourself why you take such offense even when that was not the intent. Get it out and let it go.

____

____

____

____

____

____

____

____

____

____

PRAY:

Father God, please release me from the spirit of offense and all its strongholds in my life. Lord, I command the spirit of faith and the spirit of truth to rule and reign in my life. Lord, I let go of offense and boldly stand in the strength of your truth. I rebuke the spirit of offense and rejoice in the peace you bring to my life. In Jesus's mighty name, I pray. Amen. CUT THEN BURN THESE PAGES.

DAY 22

SETTLING

It is easy to reflect on our past or look at our current situation and see where we settled for less than God's best for us. We allow our emotions, impatience, and need to control to govern our decisions and relationships. We did not wait on God nor did we seek Him. What did you settle for in your life? Are you with the person God chose for your life or not? Did you settle for the wrong job, a wrong group of friends, or even the wrong home because you moved too fast? Maybe you settled for allowing yourself to be treated badly or taken advantage of by someone you care about. Write it down and commit to stop settling in your life.

____

____

____

____

____

____

____

____

____

PRAY:

Father God, forgive me for not seeking you in all things. Forgive me for moving past you when I should have waited on you. I commit to waiting upon the Lord and seeking you in all things. I rebuke the spirit of complacency and impatience in the name of Jesus. Lord, I ask that you place in me a clean heart that will seek only what you provide to my life. I give you praise for what you have done, are doing, and will do in my life forevermore. In Jesus's mighty name, I pray. Amen. CUT THEN BURN THESE PAGES.

DAY 23

ANGER

What are you angry about? Many people will say they are not angry, not realizing they are filled with unresolved anger. Most of the time we don't realize anger is hiding underneath, unless we are faced with a memory, see someone again, or run across another type of reminder. Do you find yourself overreacting to certain people or situations? Do you feel anger and hatred toward anyone for what they did to you or someone you love? Do you say mean things not realizing that the words from your mouth are derived from your personal pain and mental anguish? Write it out here and leave it here. Search yourself for anger. Do not allow it to control your life.

____

____

____

____

PRAY:

Father God, I rebuke the spirit of anger right now. I cast my cares unto you Lord. I ask that you help me walk in peace and love instead of anger. I speak life to my spirit and command the spirit of peace to return unto me in Jesus's name. I commit my emotions to you and ask you to help me fight against this spirit of Anger now and forevermore. In Jesus's mighty name, I pray. Amen. CUT THEN BURN THESE PAGES.

DAY 24

UNFORGIVENESS

Forgiveness is not for the person who hurt you, it is for you. When you learn to forgive others, no matter how hard it may be, you release the dark cloud they left over your life. The enemy loses the power he took by the wrong done to you. Forgiveness allows the healing process to truly begin. The act of forgiving is a process that begins by speaking and/or writing the words and seeking God for strength. Write down all the things you struggle to forgive and let the healing begin today.

____

____

____

____

____

____

PRAY:

Father God, forgive me for holding on to unforgiveness. Please strengthen me so I can truly learn to walk in love and forgiveness. Lord, please help me to remember that I wrestle with spirits within them, not the flesh and blood of those who hurt me. Father, I ask for a renewing of my heart and spirit right now in the name of Jesus. I forgive all who have hurt me so that I can be truly free. Let my truth set me free and place a hedge of protection around all concerning me. In Jesus's mighty name, I pray. Amen. CUT THEN BURN THESE PAGES.

DAY 25

IDOLIZING

The word of God speaks clearly about not idolizing and serving other gods. Human beings have made Gods out of many things including people, material things, and money. In this world, it is dangerous to put any of these things before God. The pain in your life likely happens because you place people, including family, in a space where only God is meant to dwell. Then when they do something to hurt you, it is difficult to bounce back. People idolize pastors, celebrities, athletes, their children, spouses, teachers, events and so much more. What or who have you made an idol in your life? What, in your life, is more important than God? What, if it were gone tomorrow, would have a lasting and devastating effect on you?

____

____

____

____

____

____

____

____

PRAY:

Father God, please forgive me for idolizing man and material things. Father forgive me for putting things of this world before you. Lord, help me to love myself and learn to rely on you for all I need. Lord, please establish in me restraint and the mind to think before blindly doing things that cause me to sin against you. In Jesus's mighty name I pray. Amen. CUT THEN BURN THESE PAGES.

DAY 26

WISHING HARM

Even on the worst people, we are not to wish harm. In times of anger and pain, we sometimes wish people would "Get what they deserve" or we wish they would feel the pain we feel. We think that in some way enacting revenge on that person will take away our pain and heal our hearts. The only one who can do that is God. Who have you wished harm to fall upon? Who did/do you want to hurt and maybe did return evil for evil? It's time to cleanse that from your life. Write it down, sort it out, and let it go.

____

____

____

____

____

____

____

____

____

____

____

PRAY:

Father God, I repent for wishing harm on another person. Please forgive me for sinning against you in any way. Lord, I lift my eyes toward Heaven and ask that you place in me a clean heart. Lord help me to forgive and take back any power given to the enemy by my anger, unforgiveness, and hatred towards another. Heal my mind and heart in the name of Jesus. I give you the glory with my life. In Jesus's name, I pray. Amen. CUT THEN BURN THESE PAGES.

DAY 27

ENABLING

Enabling another person in the wrong way has terrible repercussions. In essence, you are telling them YOU will be strong for them, speak for them, fight for them, and even feel for them. Your actions take their power and tell them they are incapable without you necessarily speaking the words. They become dependent on you instead of seeking God for themselves. Our need to protect and defend becomes the very anchor that causes them to drown. Who have you enabled in your life? What evidence do you see? Why did you serve as a crutch rather than empowering them? How have you damaged them? Who enabled you and how?

____

____

____

____

____

____

____

____

____

PRAY:

Father God, please reverse the effects of my enabling actions and words. Forgive me for standing in the way of anyone seeking you with their whole heart. Father help me to know what to do and what not to do. Holy Spirit, lead me to empower your people and not hinder them. I rebuke the spirit of enabling from my life right now in the mighty name of Jesus. Lord restore their self-confidence and empower them today. In Jesus's name, I pray. Amen. CUT THEN BURN THESE PAGES.

DAY 28

DISABLING

Your words and actions toward others can stop them dead in their tracks and snatch their self-confidence. The words from your mouth that speak negativity and curse others have devastating long-term effects. Telling people or making them feel they are not strong, not good enough, will never amount to anything, or that they are ugly is evil. Too many have fallen victim to disabling words and actions. Who have you disabled or made feel small? What words have you spoken that made someone feel stupid, inadequate, ugly, or unworthy? Think back and be honest about what you did or said. Write it down. Free them and yourself.

____

____

____

____

____

____

____

____

____

PRAY:

Father God, I humbly ask you to forgive me for my condemning words. Lord, please reverse the effects of anything I have done to harm and disable another human being. Lord snatch my words from their minds and replace them with words of hope and love. Father help me to have more discipline and to be a light in the darkness. I rebuke the disabling spirit from my life and those I have harmed. In Jesus's name, I pray. Amen. CUT THEN BURN THESE PAGES.

DAY 29

BELIEF

Sometimes it is hard to believe. No matter how much you value your faith or love God, at times, it's hard to hold on to your faith. Some refuse to believe because they lean on their own understanding about things of the spirit rather than seeking a relationship with God. Seeds of doubt are planted when we see all the bad in the world. We allow frustration to creep in and look for answers in all the wrong places. What things have you struggled to believe but did not think you could talk to anyone about it? What do you believe about God that you have been afraid to say or even take to God for discernment and wisdom?

____

____

____

____

____

PRAY:

Father God, please forgive my unbelief. Help me to have comfort in knowing I can come to you with how I feel no matter what I feel. Father help me to have confidence in your Word and seek truth above all else. Help my eyes to stay on you and to believe even when I lack understanding. Open my mind and heart to your truth. In Jesus's mighty name, I pray. Amen CUT THEN BURN THESE PAGES.

DAY 30

UNGRATEFULNESS

Have you taken your life for granted by focusing on the losses rather than the wins no matter how small? Have you ever stopped and truly took time to be grateful for being alive in a world filled with darkness, sadness, and death all around you? Do you look at the world through eyes that see a half-empty glass or one that is half full? Do you know your whole perspective on life will change if you focus on being grateful? Do you know your mind can't focus on a negative and positive thought at the same time? Write down all the wins in your life and don't leave anything out. *You will keep this as a reminder of all you should be grateful for in your life. When you feel low, pull this out and use it to gain strength.*

____

____

____

____

____

____

____

____

PRAY:

Father God, thank you so much for all the favor you have shown me in my life. Thank you for being a strong tower and protecting me from the plans of the enemy. Lord, I honor you with my life and ask that your blessings continue to fall upon me daily. Lord help me to receive from you with a grateful heart. Forgive my selfishness and ungratefulness. I rebuke the enemy in the name of Jesus. I rededicate my life to you with humility and love right now. Thank you for who you are in my life. In Jesus's mighty name, I pray. Amen. REJOICE!

DO NOT BURN THESE PAGES. YOU DID IT! 

HOW DO YOU FEEL?

Now you have freed yourself from demons you didn't know existed within you. You should feel lighter, and your perspective should be shifted. Now you can walk in light and truth as you were purposed to do. You must live according to the Word of God, not simply read it. Invite God to be the Lord of your life and ask Him to change it for the better. He is faithful.

Sometimes the remodeling that happens when you give your life over to God by choosing His way instead of the world's way is painful. The walls must be torn down and the foundation ripped apart, but the finished product will be amazing. Your life can and will change as you rebuke evil spirits, open your spiritual eyes, and invite peace into your life. I wish you love and favor and speak blessings into your life through the power of God Almighty. May the anointing of God fall on your life.

For additional understanding of spiritual warfare in your life, read *Symphony of Darkness* and *Free Your Mind.* These are books I have written to empower people while shining a light on the hidden darkness we face in our lives. I want you to win more battles.

I wrote this poem in 2000. It represents how I felt when I only knew *of* God but had not wholly given my life over to Him.

THE STORM

My chest is tight from the pain

That crawls through my soul

Disillusioned by the dark reality of this life

Who am I?

No longer a mother, a daughter, a wife

A broken spirit still wounded by the evil of the storm

That hates my very life

Thoughts of love and laughter

Diminished by sadness and death

Mad at the strength and pride that has left

The winds and rains pursue me as I run

My lifeless spirit clutched tight in my hand

Death is a promise that somehow gives hope

Sleepless life, full of hurt and loss,

I run for the children no matter the cost

The waiting pierces my heart like a knife

The vessel I am is broken and torn

I fear what is left of me after the storm.

~Acillen

This poem is the answer to the pain of my storm. This is what God can do when you give your life over to Him.

THAT DAY

I imagine myself draped with peace on that day

When the sunbeams come forth

As the storm rolls away

My spirit relieved, my imprisoned soul free

The angels that kept me will show me their face

Tears racing, hearts smiling, embraced in His Grace

My family united, my still faith revived

Thank God for His strength for it kept me alive

Flooded with hope for the days yet to come

Praises of honor for what God has done

Thank you, sweet Jesus,

Your word will not fail

Oh Lord, Your Goodness

Through my life prevail

~Acillen

Prayer

I pray Father God, that healing takes place in the life of this reader. May they commit with their whole heart to living the life you purposed them to live. May they stand in authority, guard their heart, and watch their words every day. I pray for a powerful awakening of their spirit to who they are and what they were born to do. I pray, Father, they pursue the joy that comes only from God above and align their life with your Word, God. Lord, I ask that you place a hedge of protection around every reader who has used this journal to release themselves from the snares of the enemy. I thank you Lord and plead the blood of Jesus over everything concerning them that they grow in you and prosper in all things. In the Mighty name of Jesus, we claim the victory. Amen